HIGH ALTITUDE TRUCK EXPEDITION

HÖHENWELTREKORD MIT UNIMOG

Nach einer dreieinhalbmonatigen Umbauphase sind die beiden U 5023 bereit für den Schiffstransport nach Chile.
After three months of special modifications the two U 5023 are ready to be shipped to Chile.

Vorwort / Preface

Liebe Leser,
ich freue mich sehr, dass auf Initiative des Unimog-Museums dieser schöne Bildband entstanden ist. Zeigt er doch in eindrucksvollen Bildern den Verlauf und die Erfolge eines schwierigen Expeditionsvorhabens in Höhen von knapp unter 7.000 Metern. Höhen, die mich seit 1996 faszinieren und in denen ich seither bei der Leitung von Expeditionen immer wieder mit außergewöhnlichen Teams sowie Projektpartnern unterwegs sein und Grenzen verschieben konnte.
Für mich war und ist der wichtigste Punkt bei all unseren Vorhaben, das „einander vertrauen und sich aufeinander verlassen können“. Denn nur, wenn Vertrauen die Basis ist und jeder einzelne Projektpartner und jedes einzelne Teammitglied alles gibt, man sich selbst hinten anstellt und stattdessen auf das Wohl des Nächsten achtet, gelingen außergewöhnliche Expeditionen wie diese.
Ich bin dankbar dafür, mit allen Projektpartnern und Teammitgliedern auch 2019 ein solch starkes Band des Zusammenhalts erlebt zu haben. Ein felsenfester Zusammenhalt und ein unerschütterliches füreinander einstehen, das der Grundlage aller unserer Expeditionen, Erstbefahrungen und Extremtests folgte: Einer für alle – alle für Einen.
Vielleicht überträgt sich bei der Betrachtung des Bildbandes etwas von diesem besonderen Spirit, es würde mich sehr freuen.
Viel Freude beim Lesen und Betrachten wünscht

Ihr Matthias Jeschke

Dear reader,
I am delighted that the Unimog-Museum in Gaggenau took the initiative to create this beautifully illustrated book. The impressive pictures depict the progress and the successes of a strenuous high-altitude expedition at an elevation of approximately 7,000 meters. Since 1996, when I started leading expeditions with exceptional teams and project partners and started pushing the boundaries of what is possible, these elevations always held a fascination for me.
For me, the most important part of these expeditions was and remains the spirit of mutual trust and reliance.
Remarkable expeditions such as this one only succeed in an environment, where trust prevails, where all project partners and team members give their best, put themselves last and are committed to look out for one another.
I am grateful to have experienced such a strong bond with our project partners and team members during the 2019 expedition.
It is this unwavering team spirit and steadfast mutual support that lies at the heart of all our expeditions, first ascents and extreme tests: One for all, all for one.
I would be delighted if the pages of this book conveyed some of this extraordinary spirit.
Happy reading!

Matthias Jeschke

Eng und gefährlich: der Zugang zum Paso de San Francisco.
Narrow and dangerous: Access road to "Paso de San Francisco".

Das gemeinsame Ziel / The common goal

Nach der Errichtung von zwei Schutzhütten im Jahr 2017 auf dem höchsten Vulkan der Erde, dem Ojos del Salado in Chile, wollte das Team von Extrem Events gemeinsam mit seinen Partnern einen weiteren Beitrag zur Verbesserung der Sicherheit von Bergsteigern und Wissenschaftlern leisten. Die High Altitude Truck Expedition 2019 verfolgte dabei gleich mehrere Ziele: die Installation von Notfunkeinheiten in den vier Höhenlagern des Ojos del Salado, die wissenschaftliche Zusammenarbeit mit der Universität Atacama, die Fahrzeughöhenerprobung für weitergehende Rettungs- und Höheneinsätze sowie die Verbesserung der 2014 gesetzten Höhenrekordmarke für Trucks.
Unter der Leitung von Matthias Jeschke ist es dem Extrem Events-Einsatzteam vor Ort gelungen, die Höhenlager „Refugio Murray" (4.500 m), „Refugio Apatechta" / „Camp Atacama" (5.300 m), „Refugio Tejos" (5.850 m) und „Refugio Amistad" (6.100 m) über jeweils mit Solarstrom betriebene Funkeinheiten miteinander zu verbinden. Hierdurch wurde eine Möglichkeit der direkten Kommunikation zwischen den Höhenlagern geschaffen, die in Notsituationen wertvolle Zeit beim Ersuchen um Hilfe einspart.
Die Einstellung des Höhenweltrekords für Trucks von 2014 ist dem Extrem Events-Team mit zwei Unimog ebenfalls gelungen. Und mehr noch: Mit einem der Unimog wurde eine neue Höhenweltrekordmarke für alle motorisierten Fahrzeuge gesetzt – 6.694 m.
Kein anderes Fahrzeug weltweit ist jemals höher gefahren als der Unimog U 5023 am 13.12.2019 auf dem Ojos del Salado!

After building two mountain shelters in 2017 on the highest volcano in the world, the Ojos del Salado in Chile, the members of the German Extrem Events team and their partners wanted to further contribute to improving the safety of mountaineers and scientists. The "High Altitude Truck Expedition 2019" served various purposes: The installation of emergency radio units in the four high-altitude camps located on the Ojos del Salado volcano, the scientific cooperation with the University of Atacama, vehicle altitude testing for subsequent rescue and high-altitude operations and breaking the high-altitude record set for trucks in 2014.
Led by Matthias Jeschke, the Extrem Events team members on site managed to set up a radio communications link between the high-altitude camps "Refugio Murray" (4,500 m), "Refugio Apatechta" / "Camp Atacama" (5,300 m), "Refugio Tejos" (5,850 m) and "Refugio Amistad" (6,100 m) using 4 solar-powered emergency radio units.
The direct communication link between the camps is going to save valuable whenever emergency assistance is needed.
With their two Unimog, the Extrem Events team also broke the high-altitude world record for trucks set in 2014. At 6,694 m above sea level, one of the Unimog even set a new world record for motorized vehicles.
No other vehicle in the world ever ventured higher than the Unimog U 5023 at the Ojos del Salado on 13.12.2019.

Die beiden Special Trucks transportieren neben der Expeditionsausrüstung das Material und Werkzeug für die Installation von vier autarken Notfunkeinheiten.
Apart from expedition equipment, the two modified trucks transport material and tools for the installation of four self-contained emergency radio units.

20.11.2019 Zwischen Copiapó und erstem Höhenlager 3.500 m / En route from Copiapó to the first high-altitude camp at 3,500 m

Am 20.11.2019 verlässt das Team die Wüstenstadt Copiapó und fährt in wenigen Stunden von rund 500 m auf 3.500 m Höhe. Überwiegend geht es auf Semi-Asphalt-Straßen vorbei an vereinzelt abgelegenen Farmen der hier tief verwurzelten indigenen Bewohner, der „Colla". Mit dem Eintritt in die Abgeschiedenheit und Trockenheit der staubigen Atacama-Wüste lässt das Team alle Versorgungsquellen für Nahrung, Wasser und Treibstoff hinter sich und ist von nun an auf sich allein gestellt.

On 20.11.2019 the team leaves the desert city of Copiapó and drives from approx. 500 m above sea level to an elevation of 3,500 m within a few hours. The trucks mostly drive on semi-paved streets and pass isolated farms of indigenous people called "Colla", who are deeply rooted in the area. Upon entering the secluded, arid Atacama Desert the team leaves all sources of food, water and fuel behind. From here on out, the team members are on their own.

Teammitglied Michael Bosetti. *Team member Michael Bosetti*

Links:
Straßenabsicherungen sind kaum vorhanden und die teils sehr schmalen Straßen nicht selten von herunterstürzenden Felsbrocken beschädigt.
Left:
Crash barriers are almost non-existent. The roadways are at times extremely narrow and frequently damaged by falling rocks.

Rechts:
Auf jedes noch so schmale Tal folgt eine weite Ebene mit imposanten Bergpanoramen.
Right:
Every narrow valley leads to an open plain with an impressive panoramic views.

Ein Teil des Teams vor seiner ersten Akklimatisationswanderung. Obligatorisch: Sonnenschutz und Wasservorräte.
Part of the team prior to their first acclimatization hike. Carrying sunscreen and water supplies is mandatory.

21.11.2019 Erstes Höhenlager 3.500 m / First high-altitude camp at 3,500 m

In einer Talmulde, wo sonst Hirten ihr Lager bei ihrer Herde aufschlagen, wird das erste Höhenlager errichtet. Übernachtet wird ab jetzt zur gegenseitigen Absicherung in Zelten zu je zwei Teammitgliedern.

The team first sets up camp in a valley where shepherds usually dwell with their herds. As a precaution, two team members share a tent at camp.

Nach zwei Stunden Höhentrekking genießt das Team den Blick auf die Umgebung um das erste Höhenlager. Hier lassen sich auf etwa 3.700 m unzählige Fossilien finden.
After two hours of high-altitude trekking, the team enjoys the first panoramic views above the camp. Countless fossils can be found at an elevation of approx 3,700 m.

Internationale Straße mit Blick auf die Andenkordilleren.
International road with a view of the Andean Mountains.

Oben:
Passhöhe der Ruta 31CH,
ca. 4.100 m
Top:
At the top of the pass on Ruta 31CH
at an elevation of approx. 4,100 m

Rechts oben bis unten:
Auffahrt zur Passüberfahrt der
Ruta 31CH.
Teammitglied Daniel Müller.
Im Hintergrund: Laguna Verde.
Manuelle Betankung aus mitgeführten
Kunststoff-Spezialtanks am Straßen-
rand in ca. 4.300 m Höhe.

Right, top to bottom:
Trucks driving to the top of the pass
on Ruta 31CH.
Team member Daniel Müller.
Laguna Verde is visible in the
background.
Roadside refuelling from special
plastic tanks at an elevation
of approx. 4,300 m

23.11.2019 Zwischen erstem und zweitem Höhenlager 4.300 m / En route to the second high-altitude camp at 4,300 m

Nach drei Nächten auf 3.500 m geht es in einer Tagestour weiter zum zweiten Höhenlager an der „Laguna Verde". Mit zunehmender Höhe wird die Luft dünner und die Umgebungstemperatur nimmt trotz starker Sonnenstrahlung deutlich ab. Es gibt nur noch vereinzelt sichtbare Vegetation und das Team trifft nur noch sehr vereinzelt auf Menschen.

After three nights at 3,500 m, the team is on its way to the second high-altitude camp located at the Laguna Verde salt lake. At higher elevations, the air becomes thinner and the temperatures plummet despite the strong solar radiation. Vegetation is scarce and the team only occasionally encounters other people.

Die beiden U 5023 auf der „Carretera international" Richtung Argentinischer Grenze auf ca. 4.300 m.
The two U 5023 on the "Carretera international" close the Argentine border at about 4,300 m.

Sonnenaufgang über der Laguna Verde.
Sunrise at Laguna Verde.

25.11.2019 Zweites Höhenlager 4.300 m / Second high-altitude camp at 4,300 m

Nur wenige Meter vom Ufer der Laguna Verde wird am 27.11.2019 das zweite Höhenlager aufgeschlagen. Der türkisfarben leuchtende Salzsee liegt am Fuße des gleichnamigen Vulkans, nahe der argentinischen Grenze, und wird umrahmt von salzverkrusteten Klippen und rotsandigen Dünen. Die hier täglich auftretenden mehrstündigen Stürme, die Salz und Sand mit sich tragen, machen jeden Tag im Camp zu einer Herausforderung.

On 27.11.2019 the team is setting up camp just a few yards from the Laguna Verde shore. The turquoise-coloured salt lake, framed by salt-encrusted cliffs and red sand dunes, lies at the foot of the eponymous volcano near the Argentine border. Daily storms that last up to several hours and carry salt and sand make for challenging conditions in the camp.

Nach vier Nächten verlässt das Team am 27.11.2019 das Höhenlager Laguna Verde.
After four nights, the team leaves the Laguna Verde high-altitude camp on 27.11.2019.

Die Unimog auf ihrem Weg zum Höhenlager „Refugio Universidad de Atacama". In einer Tagesetappe fährt die Expedition von 4.300 m auf knapp 5.300 m.
The Unimog en route to the "Refugio Universidad de Atacama" camp. The team drives from 4,300 m to approx. 5,300 m in a single day.

27.11.2019 Zwischen zweitem und drittem Höhenlager 5.300 m
En route to the third high-altitude camp at 5,300 m

Mit Verlassen des Höhenlagers Laguna Verde am 27.11.2019 lässt die Expedition auch den letzten Asphalt hinter sich. Von jetzt an bestimmen Sand, Felsen, Eis und Schmelzwasser die Bodenbeschaffenheit. Die hochgeländegängigen Unimog mit der Alliance-Spezialbereifung sind jetzt voll in ihrem Element.

Upon leaving the Laguna Verde camp on 27.11.2019, the members of the expedition also leave the last paved roads behind. The terrain is made up of sand, rocks, ice and meltwater run-off. Equipped with special Alliance tyres, the off-road vehicles effortlessly take to the rough terrain.

Das Ziel vor Augen: Der Vulkan „Ojos del Saldo" mit seinen drei Gipfeln (6.893 m, 6.752 m, 6.721 m), aufgenommen auf ca. 4.600 m.
The Ojos del Salado with its three peaks (6,893 m, 6,752 m, 6,721 m) is within sight. The picture was taken at approx. 4,600 m.

Die beiden Unimog werden rückwärts aneinander gefahren und die Ladeflächen mit einer Zusatzplane zu einer multifunktionalen Räumlichkeit verbunden.
Hier die Teammitglieder Eberhard Hohm, Andreas Stahlhofer, Matthias Jeschke, Andrea Strauß und Alexandra Jeschke im Küchen-, Vorrats- und Speiseraum.
The two Unimog are parked back to back and an extra tarpaulin is thrown over the trucks' cargo areas to create a multi-purpose space.
Team members Eberhard Hohm, Andreas Stahlhofer, Matthias Jeschke, Andrea Strauß and Alexandra Jeschke gather in the kitchen, pantry and dining area.

1.12.2019 Drittes Höhenlager 5.300 m / Third high-altitude camp at 5,300 m

Das „Refugio de Universidad de Atacama“ ist das zentrale Basislager für alle, die den Ojos del Salado erklimmen wollen. Hier treffen Menschen aus allen Teilen der Welt aufeinander. Die Schutzhütte „Refugio Apacheta“ wird durch das Extrem Events-Team mit der zweiten Notfunkeinheit ausgestattet.

The “Refugio de Universidad de Atacama” is the central base camp for everyone seeking to climb the Ojos del Salado volcano. People from around the globe meet at the camp. The Extrem Events team installs the second emergency radio unit at the “Refugio Apacheta” mountain shelter.

Installation der zweiten Notfunkeinheit am „Refugio Apacheta“.
The team installs the second emergency radio unit at “Refugio Apacheta”.

Um bei extremsten Steilfahrten zusätzlichen Druck auf die Vorderachse zu bringen und damit eine noch bessere Traktion zu erreichen, wird an den Unimog je eines der Alliance-Spezialräder auf die extra dafür gefertigte Frontkonstruktion montiert.

To add additional weight to the front axle for increased traction on the steepest slopes, one of the special Alliance tyres is mounted on the Unimog's custom-built front attachment.

Unten:
Die von Teammitglied Andreas Stahlhofer eigens für die Expedition konstruierten, einzigartigen Spezialketten werden für ihren Einsatz vorbereitet und griffbereit am Heck des ersten Unimog befestigt.

Below:
Team member Andreas Stahlhofer specifically designed the unique tyre chains for this expedition. The chains are prepared for use and attached to back of the first Unimog.

Gewichtsreduktion der Fahrzeuge: Um für die anstehenden Steilpassagen bestmöglich vorbereitet zu sein, lässt das Team entbehrliches Equipment im Höhenlager „Refugio Universidad de Atacama“ zurück.
Minimizing the cargo load: To be optimally prepared for the upcoming steep slopes, the team unloads unnecessary equipment at the “Refugio Universidad de Atacama” high-altitude camp.

4.12.2019 Drittes Höhenlager 5.300 m / Third high-altitude camp at 5,300 m

Das Team bereitet sich und die beiden Trucks auf die nun anstehenden Extrempassagen vor. Nur das Notwendigste an Kleidung, Proviant und Wasser in Rationen wird auf den Unimog transportiert. Viel Ausrüstung wie Ersatzzelte, Zusatzkraftstoff und weitere Lebensmittelvorräte verbleiben zusammen mit dem Anhänger im Camp auf 5.300 m.

The team prepares itself and the two trucks for conquering the steepest passages. The Unimog only carry essential clothing, provisions and water rations. Most of the equipment, such as replacement tents, spare food and fuel supplies as well as the trailer remain at the third camp.

Bei Sonnenaufgang am 7.12.2019 sind die Unimog abfahrbereit.
On 7.12.2019 the Unimog are ready to depart at sunrise.

Um bestmögliche Bedingungen für die Auffahrt durch die Felsrinne zu schaffen, sind die Unimog jeweils nur mit dem Fahrer besetzt. Das übrige Team erklimmt samt Rucksäcken den Felskanal zu Fuß. Bis heute gibt es weltweit nur eine Handvoll Fahrzeuge und Fahrer, denen die Befahrung dieser Steilpassage gelungen ist.

To create the best possible conditions for the steep ascent through the gully, the Unimog are only manned with one driver. The rest of the team climbs the gully on foot with backpacks. To date, only a handful of vehicles and drivers successfully managed to navigate the steep passage.

7.12.2019 Zwischen drittem und viertem Höhenlager 6.100 m / En route to the fourth high-altitude camp at 6,100 m

Auf ca. 6.000 m stellen sich die Unimog, die Alliance-Reifen und das Team an einer Schlüsselstelle einer besonderen Herausforderung: Die Fahrt durch einen extrem steilen Felskanal, der von massiven Gesteinsbrocken durchzogen ist, erfordert höchste Konzentration von den Fahrern und großes Vertrauen in die beiden U 5023.
Am späten Nachmittag erreichen die Unimog und das Team wie geplant ein kleines Plateau mit der Schutzhütte „Refugio Amistad“ auf 6.100 m.

At approx. 6,000 m the Unimog, the Alliance tyreas and the team face a particularly difficult challenge: Driving through an extremely steep gully crisscrossed with massive boulders requires the drivers' utmost concentration and great confidence in the two U 5023.
By late afternoon, the Unimog and the team reach a small plateau and the “Refugio Amistad“ mountain shelter at an elevation of 6,100 m.

Auf ihrem Weg zur Felsrinne passieren die Unimog das Camp „Refugio Tejos“ auf 5.850m, wo das Team wenige Tage zuvor die dritte Notfunkeinheit erfolgreich installiert hatte.
On their ascent to the gully, the Unimog pass the “Refugio Tejos”' camp at 5,850 m, where the team successfully installed the third emergency radio unit a few days earlier.

Die beiden U 5023 bilden auch auf 6.100m wieder das Zentrum des Höhenlagers.
Once again, the two U 5023 provide a makeshift space at the high-altitude camp at 6,100 m.

Geschafft! Glücklich präsentiert sich das Team neben der fertig aufgebauten Notfunkeinheit (Solarpanel, Funkgerät- und antenne, Signalleuchte) im „Refugio Amistad".
They did it! The team happily poses for the camera next to the installed emergency radio unit (solar panel, radio, antenna, signal beacon) at "Refugio Amistad".

8.12.2019 Viertes Höhenlager 6.100 m / Fourth high-altitude camp at 6,100 m

Mit vereinten Kräften wird die letzte Notfunkeinheit erfolgreich installiert. Sie ist nun via Funk mit den anderen drei Notfunkeinheiten verbunden. Damit hat das Team ein wichtiges und wesentliches Ziel der Expedition erreicht!

In a joint effort the team successfully installs the last emergency radio unit, which provides a direct link to the three emergency radio units at the other camps. The team has reached a vital milestone of the expedition.

Vom Camp auf 6.100 m scheint der Gipfel des Ojos del Salado zum Greifen nah.
From the camp at 6,100 m the summit of the Ojos del Salado volcano seems just within reach.

Zwei der insgesamt drei Gipfel des Ojos del Salado: links der Hauptgipfel (6.893 m), in der Mitte der Zentralgipfel (6.752 m).
Two of the three Ojos del Salado mountain peaks: The main peak (6,893 m on left) is visible next to the central peak (6,752 m).

9.12.2019 Hochplateau nach viertem Höhenlager / High Plateau after the fourth high-altitude camp

Nun will es das Team wissen und lässt auch das Höhenlager „Refugio Amistad“ hinter sich: Wie hoch schaffen es die beiden U 5023? Kann das Team der weiter zunehmenden Kälte, dem Sauerstoffmangel und der Abgeschiedenheit trotzen? Zunächst gilt es am Hochplateau ein Eisfeld zu überwinden...

The team is exploring new heights and leaves the “Refugio Amistad” high-altitude camp behind. Which elevation benchmark will the two U 5023 trucks be able to reach? Can the team brave the isolation, the lack of oxygen and the increasing cold? First, they must cross an ice field at the high plateau.

Oben:
Das Eisfeld wird im Schritttempo in Angriff genommen.
Immer wieder gilt es, mit äußerster Vorsicht einen Weg durch Sand und Geröll zu finden.

Links:
Philipp Geisler, Alexandra Jeschke, Michael Bosetti, Eberhard Hohm, Daniel Müller, Andreas Stahlhofer.

Top:
The Unimog slow to a crawl to cross the ice field.
Navigating through sand and debris is challenging and requires extreme caution.

Left:
Part of the crew: Philipp Geisler, Alexandra Jeschke, Michael Bosetti, Eberhard Hohm, Daniel Müller, Andreas Stahlhofer.

Oben: Das oft scharfkantige Lavagestein kann den Alliance-Reifen nichts anhaben.
Mitte und unten links: Die Unimog zwischen Felsen und Eis.
Unten rechts: Die Unimog vor dem Hauptkrater (links) und dem Zentralen Krater (rechts).

Top: The sharp-edged lava rocks are no match for the Alliance tyres.
Middle and bottom left: The Unimog navigate through rocks and ice.
Bottom right: The Unimog with the main (left) and central craters (right) visible in the background.

Mit den letzten Sonnenstrahlen erreicht das Team die nächste Höhenmarke: 6.350 m.
As the sun is about to set, the team reaches the next elevation benchmark: 6,350 m

Oben: Die Unimog beginnen mit der Gletscherüberquerung auf 6.400 m.
Unten: Im Schritttempo und mit äußerster Vorsicht arbeiten sich die Fahrer durch das scharfkantige Gletschereis.

Top: The Unimog are heading across the glacier at 6,400 m.
Bottom: The drivers use utmost caution to work their way through the sharp ice formations.

9.12.2019 Fünftes Höhenlager und Gletscherüberquerung auf 6.400 m / Fifth high-altitude camp and glacier crossing at 6,400 m

Nach einer Übernachtung auf etwa 6.300 m wird der Aufstieg fortgesetzt: Auf dem Weg in noch größere Höhen muss das Team mit den U 5023 den zentralen Gletscher überfahren. Nicht jede Eisschicht ist tragfähig, da bereits die Winterschmelze eingesetzt hat.

After spending the night at approximately 6,300 m the team members continue their ascent. As they venture higher, the U 5023 must cross the central glacier. Since the ice already started to melt, only certain sections of the ice bear the trucks' weight.

Zur weiteren Gewichtseinsparung lässt das Team im Höhenlager 6 auch die Ersatzreifen zurück. Gewicht pro Reifen: 330 kg
To reduce the load, the team leaves the 6 spare tyres at the high-altitude camp. Each tyre weighs 330 kg.

Die Bereifung der Hinterachse eines Unimogs wird um Spezialketten ergänzt, um die Traktion auf felsig-sandigem Untergrund in Steillagen von bis zu 100% noch weiter zu erhöhen.
Special tyre chains are installed on a Unimog's rear tyres to provide additional traction on the rocky, sandy slopes with an incline of up to 100%.

Mit Warn-Spezialwinde über den Felsriegel.
The trucks drive across the rocky ridge in tandem using a Warn winch.

11.12.2019 Sechstes Höhenlager 6.450 m und Anfahrt zum siebten Höhenlager 6.640 m / Sixth high-altitude camp at 6,450 m and en route to the seventh camp at 6,640 m

Zwischen dem sechsten und siebten Höhenlager liegt ein extrem sandiger, langer und steiler Hang, der am Ende in einen Felsriegel mündet. Zur Überwindung sind beide Unimog gekoppelt und das erste Fahrzeug mit den Spezialketten ausgerüstet. Das Zurücklegen der etwa 800 m Distanz und 200 Höhenmeter dauert einen halben Tag.

En route to the seventh high-altitude camp, the team needs to conquer an extremely long, sandy and steep slope that leads to a rocky ridge. The Unimog drive up the slope in tandem, connected by a winch rope. The first vehicle is equipped with special tyre chains.Covering about 800 m and an elevation of 200 m takes half a day.

Die Windenaufnahme ist eine Sonderkonstruktion der Firma AS Baugeräte. Sie dient gleichzeitig als Aufnahme für einen Ersatzreifen.
The winch mount was custom-built by AS Baugeräte and also holds a spare tyre.

Bild unten: Auf ihrem Weg zum nächsten Zwischenziel: Gekoppelt erklimmen die Special Trucks den Steilhang.
Bottom: En route to the next destination the two trucks drive up the slope in tandem formation.

Die extrem reine Luft der Atacama Wüste bietet eine kilometerweite, beeindruckende Aussicht auf die umliegenden Fünf- und Sechstausender.
Due to the extremely clean air in the Atacama Desert, the team can see for miles and enjoys a clear view of the impressive surrounding 5,000- and 6,000-meter-high mountains.

Prüfung möglicher Fahrtrouten und Zugänge durch Matthias Jeschke.
Matthias Jeschke is scouting potential travel and access routes.

12.12.2019 Siebtes Höhenlager 6.640 m / Seventh high-altitude camp at 6,640 m

Umgeben von Steilhängen und Büßereisfeldern bilden die beiden Unimog und ein kleines Zelt das höchste Camp dieser Expedition. Es ist Ausgangspunkt für Routenerkundungen und Strategiebesprechungen.

Surrounded by steep slopes and penitentes the team sets up camp with the two Unimog and a small tent at the highest elevation to date. The camp serves as a base for strategy discussions and for scouting alternate routes.

Blick über den Zentralkraterrand auf den "Cerro Mulas Muertas" (5.878 m), hinter dem sich rechts die Laguna Verde zeigt.
View from the crater rim to "Cerro Mulas Muertas" (5,878 m) with Laguna Verde visible in the background on the right.

Rechts oben:
In Blickrichtung der Unimog liegt ein begehrtes Ziel von Wissenschaftlern: der Zentralkrater, der unaufhörlich und mit lautem Getöse vulkanische Gase ausstößt.

Mitte und unten: Äußeres Ende des Hochlagers am Kraterrand.

Top right:
The team has a direct line of sight to a destination coveted by scientists – the active central crater that thunderously and incessantly emits volcanic gases.

Middle and bottom:
Outer edge of the high-altitude camp at the crater rim.

13.12.2019 REKORDTAG 6.694 m / RECORD ATTEMPT AT 6,694 M

Laut Vorhersage steht eine ungünstige Wetterlage unmittelbar bevor. Somit trifft das Team die Entscheidung: Es versucht noch am selben Tag, mit beiden Unimog die 2014 mit einem Mercedes-Benz Zetros und Alliance-Reifen erzielte Höhenrekordmarke von 6.675 m zu überfahren.

According to the forecast, inclement weather is fast approaching. The team members reach a decision: Today, they will attempt to break the existing altitude record of 6,675 m that was set in 2014 with a Mercedes-Benz Zetros with Alliance tyres.

Links: Beide Trucks verlassen für den Rekordversuch das Höhenlager 7.

Left: Both trucks leave the seventh high-altitude camp to attempt a new world record.

Off-road Unimog.
Built for extremes

Off-road Unimog.
Built for extremes.
MATTHIAS JESCHKE

Oben:
Unüberwindbares Felsgestein stoppt die Weiterfahrt.

Oben rechts:
Ein Windenseil sichert den zweiten Unimog und wird via Fernbedienung gesteuert.
Das Team hat es geschafft: Die 2014 gesetzte Weltrekordmarke von 6.675 m ist überboten!

Top:
Insurmountable rocks prevent the ascent.

Top right:
The second Unimog is secured with the rope from the remotely controlled winch. They did it! The team surpassed the 2014 high-altitude world record of 6,675 m.

Off-road Unimog.
Built for extremes.

Oben und rechts:
Sicherheit hat höchste Priorität: Unter maximaler Anstrengung wird eine Schlinge aus LKW-Abschleppseilen um einen gigantischen Felsblock gezogen, der Unimog ist abgesichert.

Links:
Modernste Panasonic-Geräte stellen die Positionsbestimmung und die Kommunikation sicher.

Top and left:
Safety is paramount – the team members summon all their strength to loop a towing cable around a giant boulder and secure the Unimog in place.

Left:
State-of-the-art Panasonic devices are used for communication and accurate positioning.

Und es geht weiter: An einer zweiten Stelle des Steilhangs versucht das Team einen der beiden Unimog noch höher zu fahren ...

Still the team forges ahead: At a second location they try to drive one of the Unimog even higher up the slope.

Rechte Seite: Es ist geschafft, der U 5023 erreicht mit Alliance-Spezialreifen und -Ketten 6.694 m: Weltrekord.
Right: Mission accomplished! The U 5023 with its special Alliance tyres reaches 6.694 m – a new world record.

In einem ersten Versuch arbeiten sich die beiden Unimog hintereinander den Steilhang hinauf bis auf über 6.675 m. Nie zuvor haben zwei Trucks gemeinsam eine solche Höhe erklommen.

In a first attempt, the two Unimog work one after the other up the steep slope to over 6,675 m. Never before two trucks have climbed such a height together.

Endposition des ersten Höhenrekordversuchs im Unimog-Doppel.

The trucks' final tandem position after the first world record attempt.

ENDGÜLTIGE REKORDPOSITION

Datum: 13.12.2019
Ortszeit: 18:10 Uhr
max. Höhe: 6.694 m.ü.M.

FINAL RECORD POSITION

Date: 13.12.2019
Local time: 06:10 p.m.
Max. elevation: 6,694 m above sea level

EXTREM EVENTS - MATTHIAS JESCHKE
museum
MEREX
MERTEC
BTT
BOSETTI TECH TRANSFER
CNC - MACHINE TOOLS
Q-JEANS
ALLIANCE
ENGINEERED TO KEEP YOU AHEAD
ZAGRO
Group
buch
&
bild

15./16./17.12.2019 Retour / The journey back

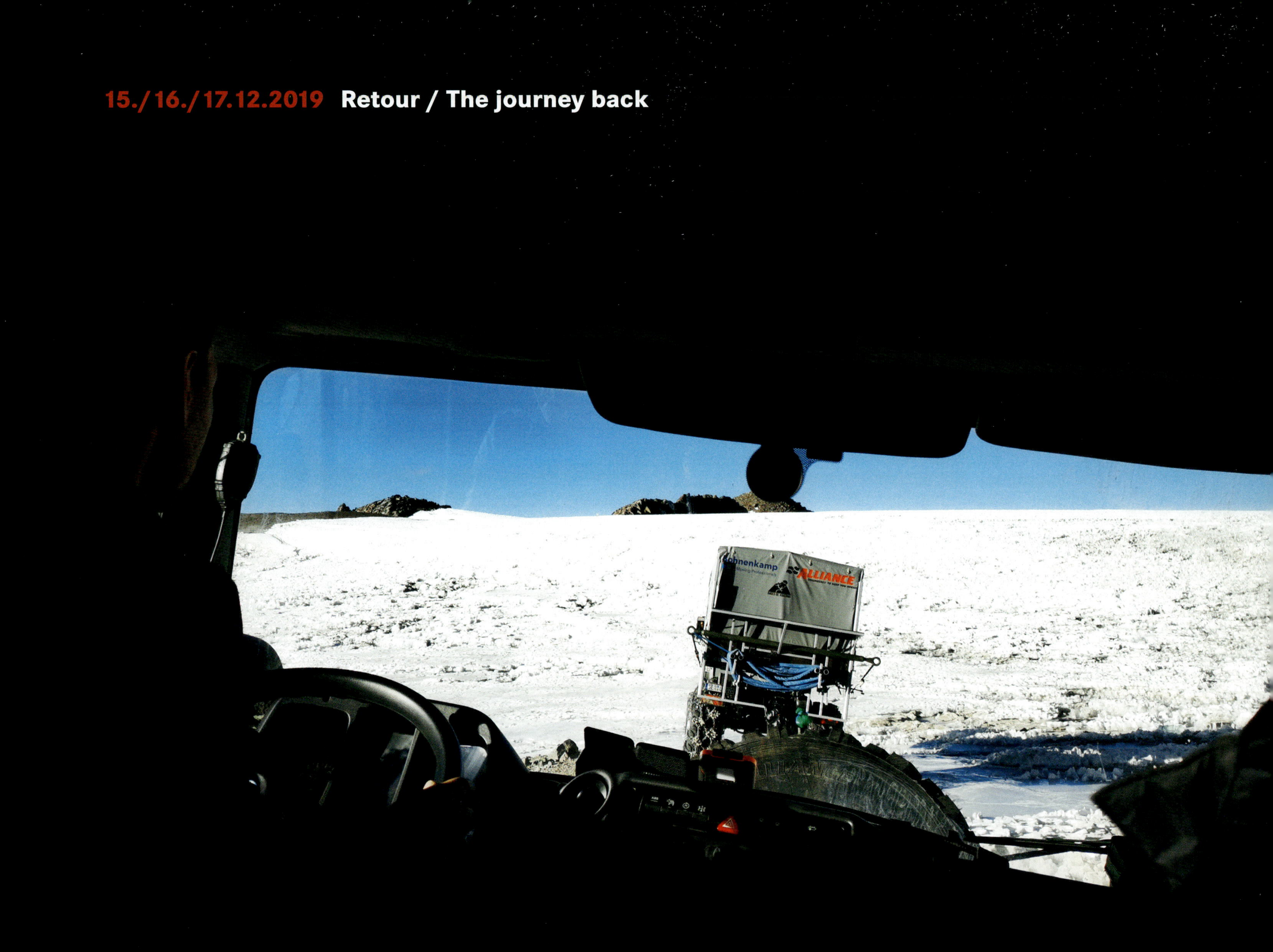

Das Team verlässt am 15.12.2019 die Gipfelregion – nur wenige Stunden vor Einsetzen eines schweren Sandsturms. Auf dem Rückweg wird alles zuvor zurückgelassene Equipment wieder vollständig aufgeladen.

On the 15th of December 2019 the team leaves the peaks behind, just a few hours prior to the onset of a heavy sandstorm. On their way back, the team collects the equipment they left at the camp.

Mit der gesamten Ausrüstung an Bord geht es zurück, auch der Spezialanhänger ist wieder dabei. Nach den Strapazen und Entbehrungen der zurückliegenden Wochen freut sich das Team auf die Zivilisation.

With the complete equipment on board and the special trailer in tow, they make their way back down. After the hardships of the past few weeks, the team is looking forward to returning to civilization.

Wo die Sonne nicht hinscheint, liegen die Temperaturen auch am Tage deutlich unter Null.
In the shade the daily temperatures remain well below zero.

Links und rechts vom Zugmaul ist zugriffsbereit je eine Spezialkette befestigt.
The tyre chains are attached to the left and right of the tow hitch for easy access.

Der OJOS DEL SALADO ist mit einer Höhe von 6.893 m der höchste aktive Vulkan der Erde und der höchste Gipfel in Chile. Er ist der zweithöchste Gipfel der westlichen Hemisphäre und einer der Seven Second Summits.
At 6,893 m the OJOS DEL SALADO is the highest active volcano on earth and the highest Chilean mountain. It is one of the "Seven Second Summits" and the second highest mountain in the Western hemisphere.

Sponsoring

unimog museum

my UNIMOG MOBILE SERVICE
#PARTOFALEGEND

EXTREM EVENTS MATTHIAS JESCHKE

ALLIANCE
ENGINEERED TO KEEP YOU AHEAD

WARN

Panasonic
TOUGHBOOK

AS Baugeräte

ZAGRO Group

Bohnenkamp
Moving Professionals

Q-JEANS®
by Mike Bosetti

MEREX MERTEC
Ihre UNIMOG-Spezialisten aus Gaggenau

UNIVERSIDAD DE ATACAMA
FACULTAD DE INGENIERÍA
Departamento de Geología

BTT
BOSETTI TECH TRANSFER
CNC - MACHINE TOOLS

ANDES DE ATACAMA
MUCHO MÁS QUE MONTAÑAS

Danke an... / Our thanks go to...

alle Partner, Unterstützer und Freunde des Projekts,
jeden Einzelnen des fantastischen Einsatzteams,
die chilenischen Behörden, den Grenzschutz und die High-Andes Polizeieinheit.

all of our partners, supporters and friends of the project,
every member of the extraordinary team, the Chilean authorities,
the Chilean border patrol and the High-Andes Police Unit.

Impressum / Publishing Information

Herausgeber: Unimog-Museum BetriebsGmbH, An der B 462, 76571 Gaggenau
info@unimog-museum.de, www.unimog-museum.com
Redaktion: Hildegard Knoop, Nina Skála
Text und Fotos: Extrem Events, Alexandra und Matthias Jeschke
Gestaltung/Layout: Klaus Dettmann

Verlag: Buch & Bild Unimog-Museum GmbH, An der B 462, 76571 Gaggenau,
office@buchundbild.de
Druck: naberDRUCK GmbH, 76549 Hügelsheim, Am Hecklehamm 1, naber@naberdruck.de

Publisher: Unimog-Museum BetriebsGmbH, An der B 462, 76571 Gaggenau
info@unimog-museum.de, www.unimog-museum.com
Editorial team: Hildegard Knoop, Nina Skála
Text and pictures: Extrem Events, Alexandra and Matthias Jeschke
Artwork: Klaus Dettmann

Publishing company: Buch & Bild Unimog-Museum GmbH, An der B 462, 76571 Gaggenau,
office@buchundbild.de
Print: naberDRUCK GmbH, 76549 Hügelsheim, Am Hecklehamm 1, naber@naberdruck.de

ISBN 978-3-00-065843-3